A Mother is Love

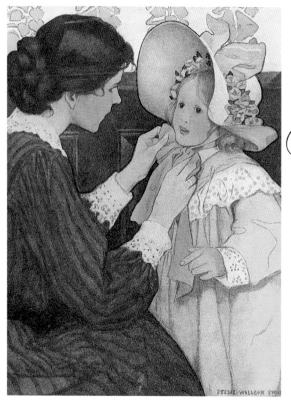

A Mother is Love

Edited by Gail Harvey

Gramercy Books

New York • Avenel, New Jersey

Introduction and Compilation
Copyright © 1992 by Outlet Book Company, Inc.
All rights reserved.
First published in 1992 by Gramercy Books
distributed by Outlet Book Company, Inc.
a Random House Company,
40 Engelhard Avenue, Avenel, New Jersey 07001

Random House
New York • Toronto • London • Sydney • Auckland

Manufactured in Hong Kong

Designed by Melissa Ring

Library of Congress Cataloging-in-Publication Data
A Mother is love.
p.   cm.
ISBN 0-517-07754-X
1. Mothers—Literary collections.   2. Mother and child—Literary
collections.
PN6071.M7M67   1992
820.8'03520431—dc20   91-39845   CIP

8 7 6 5 4 3 2

Introduction

Throughout history, poets and painters, novelists and dramatists have looked to the relationship of mother and child as an inspiration for some of their greatest works. And many of the world's outstanding writers, statesmen, artists, actors, inventors, and scientists have extolled the virtues of their own mothers and proudly acknowledged their lifelong influence.

A Mother is Love is a collection of memorable tributes to mothers. Abraham Lincoln, for example, writes: "All that I am or hope to be, I owe to my angel mother." Thomas Alva

Edison, Charlie Chaplin, and Marc Chagall also attribute their success to their mothers. Winston Churchill, Florence Nightingale, Marie Antoinette, and Hans Christian Andersen write of their admiration for their mothers. Included, too, is a touching Christmas letter from Louisa May Alcott to her mother and poems by such writers as Thomas Moore, James Whitcomb Riley, Edgar Allan Poe, and Robert Louis Stevenson.

This charming book, with delightful illustrations, many by Jessie Willcox Smith, is a celebration of mothers and motherhood. It will surely be treasured and read and reread by every mother who receives it.

GAIL HARVEY

New York
1992

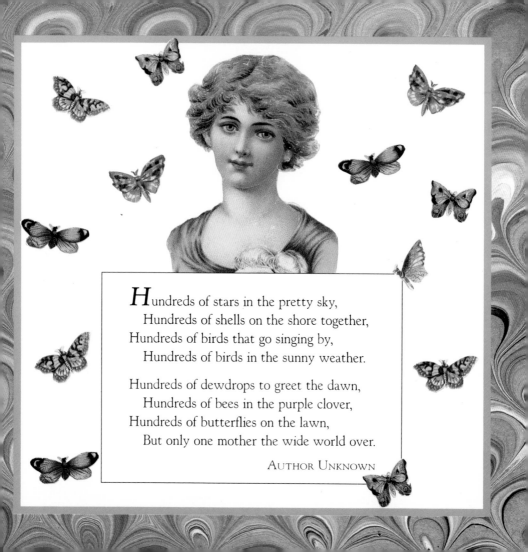

*H*undreds of stars in the pretty sky,
   Hundreds of shells on the shore together,
Hundreds of birds that go singing by,
   Hundreds of birds in the sunny weather.

Hundreds of dewdrops to greet the dawn,
   Hundreds of bees in the purple clover,
Hundreds of butterflies on the lawn,
   But only one mother the wide world over.

AUTHOR UNKNOWN

JESSIE WILLCOX SMITH

*O*h, baby, baby, baby dear,
We lie alone together here;
The snowy gown and cap and sheet
With lavender are fresh and sweet;
Through half-closed blinds the roses peer
To see and love you, baby dear.

We are so tired, we like to lie
Just doing nothing, you and I,
Within the darkened quiet room.
The sun sends dusk rays through the gloom,
Which is no gloom since you are here,
My little life, my baby dear.

Soft sleepy mouth so vaguely pressed
Against your new-made mother's breast.
Soft little hands in mine I fold,
Soft little feet I kiss and hold,
Round soft smooth head and tiny ear,
All mine, my own, my baby dear.

E. NESBIT

With a mother of different mental caliber

I would probably have turned out badly.

Thomas Alva Edison, American inventor,
about his mother Nancy Elliott Edison

It was from you that I first learned to think, to feel, to imagine, to believe. . . .

John Sterling, nineteenth-century British
essayist and poet, in his last letter to his
mother, who died a week later

A man who has been the indisputable favorite of his mother keeps for life the feeling of a conqueror, that confidence of success that often induces real success.

Sigmund Freud, the
founder of psychoanalysis

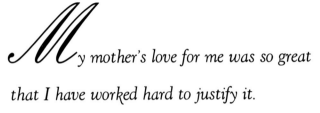

My mother's love for me was so great

that I have worked hard to justify it.

Painter Marc Chagall, just before his
ninetieth birthday

My mother gave me to the moons,
And gave in turn the moons to me,
One midnight when she sang her tunes
To a baby on her knee.

HANIEL LONG

JESSIE WILLCOX SMITH 1907

It seems to me that my mother was the most splendid woman I ever knew. . . . I have met a lot of people knocking around the world since, but I have never met a more thoroughly refined woman than my mother. If I have amounted to anything, it will be due to her.

Charles Chaplin, British actor and producer

A mother is a mother still,
The holiest thing alive.

SAMUEL TAYLOR COLERIDGE

MY MOTHER'S GARDEN

*H*er heart is like her garden,
Old-fashioned, quaint and sweet,
With here a wealth of blossoms,
And there a still retreat.
Sweet violets are hiding,
We know as we pass by,
And lilies, pure as angel thoughts,
Are opening somewhere nigh.

Forget-me-nots there linger,
To full perfection brought,
And there bloom purple pansies
In many a tender thought.
There love's own roses blossom,
As from enchanted ground,
And lavish perfume exquisite
The whole glad year around.

And in that quiet garden—
The garden of her heart—
Songbirds are always singing
Their songs of cheer apart.
And from it floats forever,
O'ercoming sin and strife,
Sweet as the breath of roses blown,
The fragrance of her life.

ALICE E. ALLEN

My mother always seemed to me a fairy princess, a radiant being possessed of limitless riches and power. . . .

Winston Churchill, British statesman and prime minister

$\mathscr{R}$emember there is no one to whom

I shall be prouder to tell of my successes or

more willing to confess my failures.

Robert Falcon Scott, Antarctic explorer, in
a letter written in October 1911 to his
mother from the winter quarters of the
British Antarctic Expedition

When little Elizabeth whispers
    Her morning-love to me,
Each word of the little lisper's,
    As she clambers on my knee—
Hugs me and whispers, "Mommy,
    Oh, I'm so glad it's day
    And the night's all gone away!"
How it does thrill and awe me,—
    The night's all gone away!

"And oh," she goes eerily whining
    And laughing, too, as she speaks,
"If only the sun kept shining
    For weeks and weeks and weeks!—
For the world's so dark, without you,
    And the moon's turned down so low—
    'Way in the night, you know,—
And I get so lonesome about you!—
    'Way in the night, you know!"

JAMES WHITCOMB RILEY

JESSIE WILLCOX SMITH

*W*hatever beauty or poetry is to be found in my little book is owing to your interest in and encouragement of all my efforts from the first to the last, and if ever I do anything to be proud of, my greatest happiness will be that I can thank you for that, as I may do for all the good that is in me.

Louisa May Alcott, American writer, in a
Christmas letter to her mother in 1854
accompanying a copy of her first book,
Flower Fable

Living with her was like being on a

journey of discovery that never ended.

Elizabeth Goudge, British novelist, about
her mother

I should be as happy here as the day is long, if I could hope that I had your smile, your blessing, your sympathy upon it. . . .

Florence Nightingale, British nurse, in a
letter to her mother from a nurses' training
institute in Dusseldorf

Who ran to help me when I fell,
And would some pretty story tell,
Or kiss the place to make it well?
My mother.

ANN TAYLOR

BESSIE WILLCOX SMITH.

In afterlife you may have friends, fond, dear friends, but never will you have again the inexpressible love and gentleness lavished upon you which none but a Mother bestows.

Thomas Babington Macaulay, nineteenth-century English historian, author, and statesman

Half an orphan is the fatherless child;

a whole orphan, the motherless.

Finnish Proverb

You have tangible wealth untold;
Caskets of jewels and coffers of gold.
Richer than I you can never be—
I had a mother who read to me.

STRICKLAND GILLILAN

I wish I could go on writing to you, it's so consoling. . . . I can't call for more of your sympathy than you will give, can I? Oh Mother, Mother.

Gertrude Bell, British traveler,
archaeologist, and government official, to
her beloved stepmother

I assure you that I have never received one of your dear letters without regretting, with tears in my eyes, that I am separated from such a tender and good mother, and though I am happy enough here, I still ardently wish that I could return to see my dear, my very dear family. . . .

Marie Antoinette, doomed French queen, to her mother, Maria Theresa, Empress of Austria

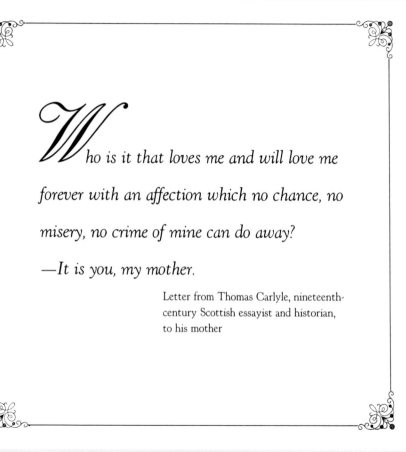

Who is it that loves me and will love me forever with an affection which no chance, no misery, no crime of mine can do away?

—It is you, my mother.

Letter from Thomas Carlyle, nineteenth-
century Scottish essayist and historian,
to his mother

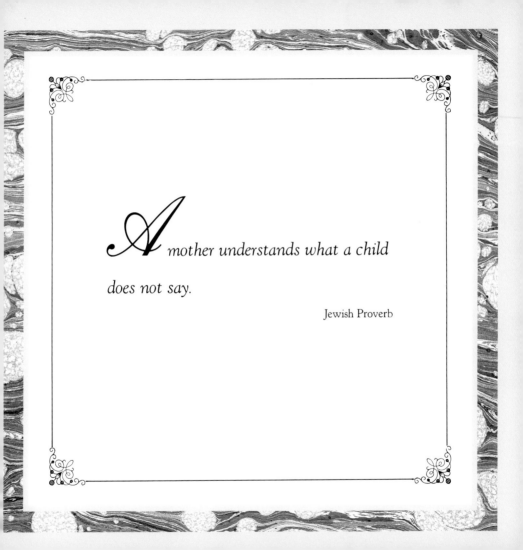

A mother understands what a child does not say.

Jewish Proverb

Nobody knows of the work it makes
   To keep the home together,
Nobody knows of the steps it takes,
   Nobody knows—but mother.

Nobody listens to childish woes,
   Which kisses only smother;
Nobody's pained by naughty blows,
   Nobody—only mother.

Nobody knows of the sleepless care
   Bestowed on baby brother;
Nobody knows of the tender prayer,
   Nobody—only mother.

Nobody knows of the lessons taught
   Of loving one another;
Nobody knows of the patience sought,
   Nobody—only mother.

Nobody knows of the anxious fears,
   Lest darlings may not weather
The storm of life in after years,
   Nobody knows—but mother.

AUTHOR UNKNOWN

Never shall I forget the thousand acts of kindness and affection I have received from you from my earliest to my latest days.

Walter Savage Landor, nineteenth-century
English poet and prose writer, to his
mother

TO MY MOTHER

They tell us of an Indian tree,
  Which howsoe'r the sun and sky
May tempt its boughs to wander free,
  And shoot and blossom wide and high,
Far better loves to bend its arms
  Downward again to that dear earth,
From which the life that fills and warms
  Its grateful being, first had birth.

'Tis thus, tho' wooed by flattering friends,
  And fed with fame (if fame it be)
This heart, my own dear mother, bends,
  With love's true instinct back to thee.

THOMAS MOORE

My mother had a great deal of trouble

with me, but I think she enjoyed it.

Samuel Clemens, who wrote under the
pseudonym Mark Twain

*I*n the Heavens above,
The angels, whispering to one another,
Can find, among their burning terms of love,
None so devotional as that of
  "Mother"

EDGAR ALLAN POE

JESSIE WILLCOX SMITH.

TO MY MOTHER

Υou too, my mother, read my rhymes
For love of unforgotten times,
And you may chance to hear once more
The little feet along the floor.

ROBERT LOUIS STEVENSON

She was ignorant of life and the world,

but possessed a heart full of love.

Hans Christian Andersen, the Danish author,
about his mother

I must send you another birthday greeting and tell you how much I love you; that with each day I learn to extol your love and your worth more, and that when I look back over my life, I can find nothing in your treatment of me that I would alter.

Louis Dembitz Brandeis, American Supreme
Court Justice, to his mother

You have been the best mother and I believe the best woman in the world.

Dr. Samuel Johnson, eighteenth-
century English lexicographer, critic,
and conversationalist

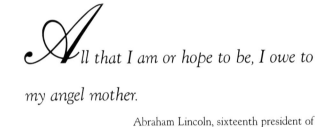

All that I am or hope to be, I owe to my angel mother.

Abraham Lincoln, sixteenth president of
the United States

She brings the sunshine into the house; it is now a pleasure to be there.

Cecil Beaton, English photographer and designer, about his mother

Fifty-four years of love and tenderness and crossness and devotion and unswerving loyalty. Without her I could only have achieved a quarter of what I have achieved, not only in terms of success and career, but in terms of personal happiness. . . . She has never stood between me and my life, never tried to hold me too tightly, always let me go free. . . .

Noel Coward, British dramatist, about his mother

M.E.GRAY.

God made a wonderful mother,
A mother who never grows old;
He made her smile of the sunshine,
And He molded her heart of pure gold;
In her eyes He placed bright shining stars,
In her cheeks, fair roses you see;
God made a wonderful mother,
And He gave that dear mother to me.

PAT O'REILLY

Women know
The way to rear up children (to be just)
They know a simple, merry, tender knack
Of tying sashes, fitting baby-shoes,
And stringing pretty words that make no sense,
And kissing full sense into empty words.

ELIZABETH BARRETT BROWNING

*N*o one but she could have brought about unity, even harmony, in a family of such strikingly varied personalities. She was the acknowledged head of the household.

Svetlana Alliluyeva, Stalin's daughter, about her mother

Mothers are the queerest things!
 'Member when John went away,
All but mother cried and cried
 When they said good-by that day.
She just talked, and seemed to be
 Not the slightest bit upset—
Was the only one who smiled!
 Others' eyes were streaming wet.

But when John come back again
 On a furlough, safe and sound,
With a medal for his deeds,
 And without a single wound,
While the rest of us hurrahed,
 Laughed and joked and danced about,
Mother kissed him, then she cried—
 Cried and cried like all git out!

EDWIN L. SABIN

Always a "little boy" to her,
  No matter how old he's grown,
Her eyes are blind to the strands of gray,
  She's deaf to his manly tone.
His voice is the same as the day he asked,
  "What makes the old cat purr?"
Ever and ever he's just the same—
  A little boy to her.

Always a "little boy" to her,
  And to him she's the mother fair,
With the laughing eyes and the cheering smile
  Of the boyhood days back there.
Back there, somewhere in the midst of years—
  Back there with the childish joy,
And to her he is never the man we see,
  But always "her little boy."

AUTHOR UNKNOWN

She was the last of the generation of real grandmothers. One of the women who made a special grace of age.

Helen Hayes, American actress, about her
maternal grandmother